This Morning

BY ALYSSA KREKELBERG

We walked in the woods this morning.

We ran this morning.

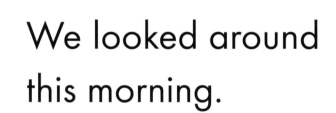

We looked around
this morning.

We saw a robin
this morning.

The robin fed its babies this morning.

We saw a brown rabbit
this morning.

We walked by the
water this morning.

We saw a duck
this morning.

We saw flowers
this morning.

Then we went home
this morning.

Note to Caregivers and Educators

Sight words are a foundation for reading. It's important for young readers to have sight words memorized at a glance without breaking them down into individual letter sounds. Sight words are often phonetically irregular and can't be sounded out, so readers need to memorize them. Knowing sight words allows readers to focus on more difficult words in the text. The intent of this book is to repeat specific sight words as many times as possible throughout the story. Through repetition of the words, emerging readers will recognize, and ideally memorize, each sight word. Memorizing sight words can help improve readers' literacy skills.

morning

this

About the Author

Alyssa Krekelberg is a children's
book editor and author. She
lives in Minnesota and enjoys
exploring the great outdoors with
her hyper husky.

Published by The Child's World®
1980 Lookout Drive • Mankato, MN 56003-1705
800-599-READ • www.childsworld.com

Photographs ©: Monkey Business Images/Shutterstock Images, cover,
1, 3, 4, 7, 15, 20; Tony Campbell/Shutterstock Images, 8, 11; Damian
Kuzdak/iStockphoto, 12; Bobkov Evgeniy/Shutterstock Images, 16;
Artsiom Malashenko/iStockphoto, 19; iStockphoto, 23

ISBN 9781503835696
LCCN 2019943126

Printed in the United States of America